cover photograph   Hand coloured by George Baxendale

back cover   Photographs by
T J Edgington/Colour Rail

first published   THE BLUECOAT PRESS
1992   Bluecoat Chambers
School Lane
Liverpool L1 3BX

typesetting: Typebase Limited
design: Michael March
print: Dah Hua Printing Press

Reprinted 1998

ISBN 1 872568 05 X

This book is dedicated to the late H C Casserley, a doyen amongst railway historians. He will be greatly missed.

Special thanks are due to Mrs G Box, who kindly made available all her late husband's material; their worth is self-evident throughout the book. Thanks also to J D Gomersall, who had the vision to photograph the line extensively during its last few months of operation and beyond. His work is published here for the first time.

I am also indebted to the following:

A W Burgess, H C Casserley,
R M Casserley, A J Cook, A G Ellis,
J W Gahan, R Gell, K W Green, B Hilton,
J B Horne, E A Livesey, K Longbottom,
B Matthews, J A Peden, G H Platt,
H B Priestley, M G Stewart, T Wright,
Liverpool City Engineer's Department,
Liverpool City Libraries, Liverpool Daily
Post and Echo and Photomatic.

The route maps have been reproduced from Bartholomew's 1928 Pocket Atlas of Liverpool, with suitable enhancements. They are divided into quarter mile squares.

Suggested further reading:
'Seventeen Stations to Dingle'
J W Gahan (1982).
'Liverpool Overhead Railway'
C E Box (1959).

THE DOCKER'S UMBRELLA

A HISTORY OF LIVERPOOL OVERHEAD RAILWAY

PAUL BOLGER

THE BLUECOAT PRESS

4

INTRODUCTION

The 'Docker's Umbrella' was not just any railway, it was an institution, an unforgettable experience for those fortunate enough to have travelled on it. Liverpudlians mourn many of the city's lost landmarks but none more so than the Liverpool Overhead Railway.

Today, the Albert Dock complex is Liverpool's undisputed main attraction but just imagine had the Overhead survived to serve it – how they would have complemented each other!

Forced to close because the cost of necessary repairs was estimated to be an unattainable two million pounds, the last trains rumbled on Sunday, December 30th, 1956, witnessed by disbelieving crowds along the line. All attempts to save it failed and the demolition men moved in on 23rd September, 1957. By January 1959, it had been felled throughout and another chapter of Liverpool's history was complete.

Being realistic, had the money been found for refurbishment it is doubtful that the Railway would have survived much beyond the 1960's. The decline of dock traffic and subsequent loss of mariners, dockers and other service personnel would have hit the Overhead's receipts severely. Consider also the wholesale migration caused by the demolition of nearby housing and the increasingly affordable motor car; the line would have found itself isolated from all but the most determined of users.

Thanks to the camera, we are able to appreciate the unique experience the Overhead Railway offered its many passengers. The photographs reproduced in this book will, it is hoped, rekindle fond memories and, for those too young to remember, give a clearer idea of what the 'Docker's Umbrella' was all about.

Paul Bolger, 1992

The opening of Liverpool Overhead Railway, 1893.

A BRIEF HISTORY

By the 1880's, Liverpool's dock network was virtually complete. So too was the congestion along the Dock Road, as carriages, omnibuses, lorries, carts and drays all plied the route. Numerous railway crossings which connected goods stations and dockside lines only added to the confusion. The passenger service had improved with the introduction of the Curtiss System, by which modified omnibuses could use Dock Board rails and revert to the road to overtake obstructions such as wagons. However, with increasing trade, the strangulation returned and it became clear that passenger traffic had to be isolated from the cargo routes in the interest of efficiency.

An elevated railway had been proposed as early as 1852 but came to nothing. It emerged again, in 1877, when the Mersey Docks and Harbour Board sought permission for a single line with passing loops at stations. This was rejected as being insufficient to meet the likely needs of the rapidly growing port but, five years later, an improved scheme did receive sanction. Unfortunately, at that time, the company had reveiwed its policy towards transporting the public and, once again, nothing was done. Finally, in 1888, a prominent group of businessmen formed the Liverpool Overhead Railway Company and obtained the Dock Board's powers by an Act of Transfer. Two leading engineers, Sir Douglas Fox and James Henry Greathead, were commissioned to design the railway and work commenced in October 1889.

Amongst the many problems encountered was the decision as to motive power. Steam was considered too dangerous to the many flammable cargoes within range of locomotive sparks.

This was one of the reasons electric traction was chosen, in 1891; other advantages being economy, speed, cleanliness and quiet running. Work was completed in January, 1893, and the line was formally opened on February 4th that year by the Marquis of Salisbury. Public transport commenced on March 6th.

The Overhead was the world's first electric elevated railway and the first to be protected by electric automatic signals. The line stretched from the Seaforth Carriage Shed to Herculaneum Dock, with public services beginning and terminating at Alexandra Dock in the north. There were eleven intermediate stations at Brocklebank, Canada, Sandon, Clarence, Princes, Pier Head, James Street, Custom House, Wapping, Brunswick and Toxteth. However, it was soon found that receipts outside working hours were poor and a decision was taken to extend the line

and to tap residential areas. A short extension to Seaforth sands was opened on April 30th, 1894, followed by another to Dingle on December 21, 1896.

The southern extension necessitated a new station at Herculaneum, the old one becoming a much needed carriage shed. Dingle (Park Road) was reached by spanning the Cheshire Lines goods yard with a 200 foot lattice girder bridge and by boring a half-mile tunnel through the sandstone high ground further inland. Thus the Overhead belied its name at the southern terminus, passengers new to Dingle no doubt wondering why they had to descend steps and a subway to gain the platforms of an elevated railway!

Langton Station was added in about 1896, only to close in 1906. Sandon was the first station to close, in 1896, being replaced by additional stations north

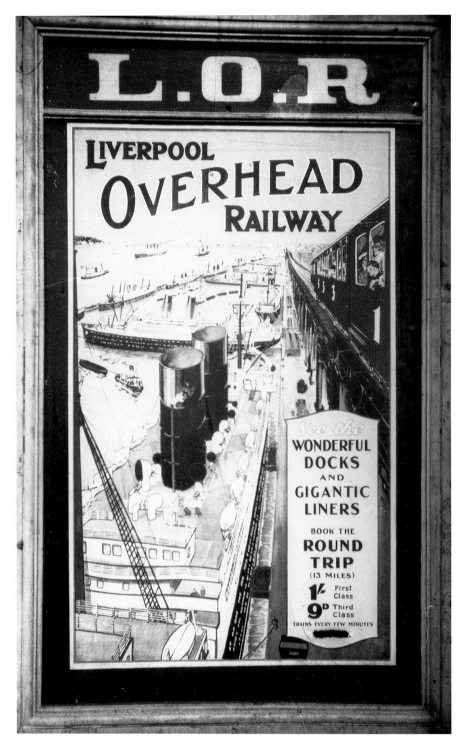

and south of it at Huskisson and Nelson.

In 1901, what is generally accepted as only the second escalator in the country was installed at Seaforth Sands. The 'Reno' moving staircase was removed in 1906, largely due to the long skirts of the day snagging in the exposed machinery, resulting in claims against the company. On July 2, 1905, a further extension was opened to the Lancashire and Yorkshire Railway's station at Seaforth and Litherland. It was now possible for travellers to access the Overhead by changing trains on the Liverpool to Southport line, which had itself been electrified the previous year. To accommodate this extra traffic, a through station was built at Seaforth Sands alongside the terminus. Both remained in use until the closure of the earlier structure, in 1925, when it was dismantled and the site used to build a replacement carriage shed (the company's original stabling point at the northern end stood in the way of construction of Gladstone Dock and had to be removed).

For a time, the Lancashire and Yorkshire Railway ran a through service from Southport to Dingle but it was discontinued in 1914. The extension to Seaforth and Litherland brought Overhead trains parallel with the LYR North Mersey branch and a junction between the two was added in 1906. This gave the Overhead access to the LYR station at Aintree Sefton Arms and a service between there and Dingle began the same year. It was not long-lived, the service being withdrawn in 1908 for all but the Aintree Races trains.

The last addition to the Overhead was the opening of a station at Gladstone on June 16, 1930, to serve the dock of the same name. Extensive bomb damage was inflicted during the Blitz but it was quickly repaired to maintain the smooth running of the docks. However, Princes Dock Station closed on March 13, 1941, due to enemy action and never reopened. Following the destruction of the Custom House building as a result of fire-bombing, it was considered appropriate to re-name its station Canning, in 1945.

Modernisation of some of the nineteen 3-car sets had begun as the War drew to a close and eight were in operation by 1955. In the same year, the curved deck plates which supported the track were reported as being in need of replacement at an approximate cost of two million pounds. This was beyond the financial resources of the company, who looked to the City Council and the Mersey Docks and Harbour Board for assistance. No adequate solution could be found and, despite rigorous public protests, the railway closed on December 30th, 1956. Rescue attempts continued until Sepember, 1957, when the dismantlers moved in.

After little more than sixty years existence, a much-loved, pioneering railway was rapidly removed from its prominent elevated position which had thrilled so many passengers with its unforgettable sights of dockland activity. Today, only traces can be seen in the form of columns set into the dock wall at Wapping, the tunnel portal at Herculaneum and the excavation at Dingle Station, now used by an engineering firm.

A JOURNEY ON THE OVERHEAD RAILWAY

The following pages describe a journey from Seaforth and Litherland to Dingle by means of photographs and captions. Along the way, we will alight to take in landmarks and other points of interest.

To facilitate this, fellow travellers must be prepared to go back and forth in time to accommodate views from different decades.

1936 Clutching our tickets, we ascend to the platforms at Seaforth and Litherland, which is on the busy Liverpool and Southport commuter line. Of the four platforms, the connecting Overhead trains always use the west side of the island platform. Approaching the latter, a fingerboard under the clock points 'TO OVERHEAD TRAINS'

1955 Walking beyond the train and turning about, we see that the platform opposite has gone; it burned down during a wartime bombing raid.

1930's A clatter behind indicates our train has been given the 'all clear' on the branch signal. The Overhead connection can be seen veering sharply to the right by the signal box.

1938 Behind is the overall view of our point of departure.

1930's As the train rounds the curve and climbs towards Rimrose Junction, we note that we have mistakenly boarded a first class coach. Generously upholstered seats, arm rests, a No Smoking compartment beyond; amongst the adverts for the White Star Line, there is a notice 'Spitting Prohibited' (as if we would!).

1950's The scatter of wheels over points heralds the passing of Rimrose Junction and the momentum eases as the train approaches Seaforth Sands. There is much to see here so it will be necessary to break journey and survey the scene.

November, 1956 Upon alighting at Seaforth Sands, we notice that the building on our platform is newly built, its predecessor having been engulfed in a fire in February. It occurred overnight and arson was suspected, the remains of an old tyre being found in one of the two trains stabled there. The total damage was estimated at £30,000, a considerable amount at that time and enough to buy fifteen semi-detached houses outright.

1923 Descending the staircase to street level and with our backs to Crosby Road South, we see that much of Fort Road is in the shadow of the railway. The covered footbridge connects the through platforms (left) with the original terminal building, which is still in use although its days are numbered. Advertisements tempt us with excursion tickets to the Wirral and August 20th sees a new comedy, 'Blinkers', at the Shakespeare Theatre in Liverpool. Cinema posters offer the latest 'flicks' at the Scala, Coliseum, Corona and Pavilion. Talkies have yet to be invented and Hal Roach is still four years away from producing regular Stan and Ollie films.

1894 Staying in the same place but going back even further in time, to the year the extension to Seaforth Sands opened. The escalator was not installed until 1901.

1923 These photographs were taken just two years before the site became a carriage shed. The absence of trains is not unusual, this part of Seaforth Sands only being used at peak times. To catch a train, it is necessary to take the footbridge across Fort Road and negotiate the staircase to the 'up' (southbound) line.

1956 Whilst traversing the footbridge, a glance to the left shows the Crosby Road South/Seaforth Road junction below.

1956 Regaining the 'up' platform, we board the modernised train which has terminated here; not all services continued to the Southport line. In two minutes, it will restart for Dingle and take us on the first leg of the Overhead proper.

1930's Taking seats at the rear of the train gives a view of Seaforth Sands from the direction of the docks. Note the diminutive signal cabin right of centre.

1894 A little further on, with a driver's view of the track. Note the conductor rails in the centre of the track. After July 1905, current was collected from rails in the six foot way to comply with the LYR system, allowing the latter's vehicles to run through to Dingle.

1894 Rounding the curve above Shore Road, another glance behind shows a bow-string bridge has just been crossed. The sidings on the right form part of the carriage depot.

1924 Keeping our eyes fixed to the rear, the carriage shed soon comes into view.

1930's Moving on in time, the carriage shed has made way for Gladstone Dock and Cunard's new liner, 'Mauretania'.

1930's A few hundred yards on Gladstone Dock station is reached, a popular sojourn for shipping enthusiasts. The LMS North Mersey & Alexandra Docks Goods Station prevents exit on the landward side so we are obliged to use one of the two foot-bridges specifically provided for access and egress.

1930's One of the ships at the dockside is Canadian Pacific's 20,000 tonner 'Duchess of Bedford', renamed 'Empress of France' after a refit in 1948.

1930's Resuming the journey, we head back to Gladstone Station.

1930's A guard's view of Gladstone and both footbridges.

1930's The train rounds the curve near Strand Road and pulls into Alexandra. Prior to the extension to Seaforth Sands, in 1894, this was the most northerly station on the line.

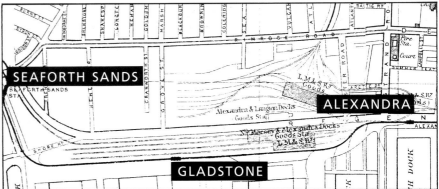

1950's Passing the site of Langton (closed in 1906), the next station reached is Brocklebank.

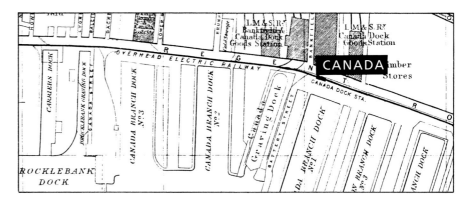

1932 The next stop is Canada Dock, with the masssive LMS Canada Goods Warehouse dominating the background.

1940 Moving on to December, 1940, with a view of bomb damage south of Canada Dock Station. The crater shows a direct hit which resulted in the loss of two complete spans.

1930's A footbridge over the line at Huskisson gives excellent views. Our attention is drawn to a man on the opposite platform who is furtively looking below and making notes. He suddenly shouts, 'Right you lot! I'm stopping an hour each, get back to work!' Foremen often had to gain height to spot 'skivers' playing cards in the high-sided railway wagons on the dock estate. The ships appear to be nudging the platform, yet there are actually seven lines of railway between the structure and the quayside.

1930's A view from the footbridge of Huskisson Station and the line to the north.

1930's Returning to the 'up' platform, we are invaded by a school party who file over the bridge for the Seaforth train. A poster (left of centre) advertises greyhound racing at Seaforth, referring to a track on Crosby Road South which operated between 1933 and 1966.

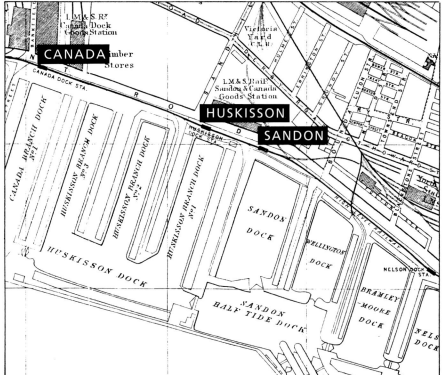

1930's Leaving Huskisson, a backwards glance shows the overall scene and our previous raised standpoint.

1930's After passing the site of Sandon Station (closed in 1896), the train gathers speed and begins a descent of 1 in 40 to take it underneath the Bramley-Moore Dock high level railway, which was established as early as 1855. This part of the Overhead is commonly called the 'switch-back' for reasons which will be obvious. (The high level line was a spur from the LYR North Docks branch and allowed coal to be tipped from wagons into vessels at the quayside).

1930's We are now at ground level and rush under the bridge to confront the gentler 1 in 80 incline to Nelson, the treading of ballasted trackwork sounding noticeably different from the the metallic rumbling which has accompanied us since Seaforth Sands.

1950's Nelson Dock Station stands on top of the 1 in 80 rise, which acts as a gravitational brake for 'up' trains.

1956 The next stop is Clarence Dock. Detraining here will allow us to inspect Stanley Dock and the surrounding area.

1920 The landward platform at Clarence affords an excellent view of Saltney Street and the massive Mersey Docks and Harbour Board's tobacco warehouse. Note the tenements, the woman toting a jug to the nearby 'Palatine' public house and the groups of hopeful dockers waiting for an opportunity to work.

1930's A rare glimpse of the Stanley Dock dual swing and lift bridge half open. The upper deck carried the Overhead lines with Dock Board rails below. Large vessels needing passage to or from the landward dock required both halves swung open but most traffic could pass underneath when the lower deck central portions were raised through 35 degrees. This composite feature meant that Overhead services were not disrupted by the majority of sailings.

1956 Regaining Clarence, a modernised 3-car set (28-9-26) arrives to take us on the next leg to Princes Dock. The 'King's pipe' chimney is just visible, on the right, beyond the road lift bridge. This was the outlet for the furnace which destroyed any sub-standard tobacco landed.

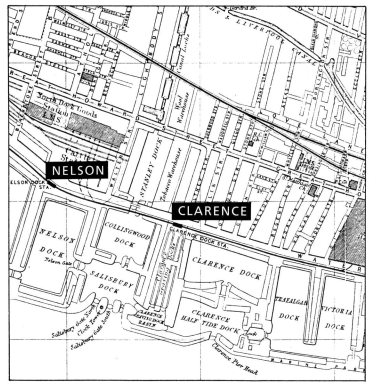

c.1900 Arriving at Princes, the train has been transformed to a single car of original stock.
Disembarking allows us to sample the atmosphere at ground level with a walk to Pier Head.

1950's A fine drizzle descends, so we take advantage of the 'umbrella' for a while, near the north end of Princes Dock transit shed. Looking north, a boilerless MDHB loco can be seen with its saddle-type water tank placed on a trolley nearby. Note too the signal (top centre) with illuminated aspect.

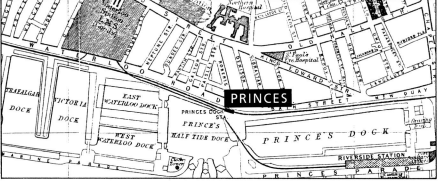

1959 The sound of steam turns our attention to the dock road, where a 'Sentinel' wagon and trailer of the United Africa Company have just come to a halt. These curious hybrids of railway engine and road lorry were a common sight in docklands up to the 1960's.

1950's Re-entering the dock estate, we walk alongside the railway towards Pier Head; lining the route are vehicles of all descriptions laden with barrels, carboys, bails and crates. The transit shed, which stands between us and the Irish boats is a hive of activity with men, machines and horses moving goods to and fro.

1950's Having received a 'ticking off' from the policeman on Princes Dock gate for our unauthorised stroll, we emerge in St Nicholas' Place and admire the commanding bow-string bridge across the roadway.

1893 Turning the clock back to the year the Overhead opened, the Liver Buildings are still eighteen years from construction, which gives an unobstructed view of the river side of Pier Head Station. Note the second bow-string bridge and the monopoly of horse-drawn traffic (electric trams were not employed until 1898).

1956 Walking underneath the line brings us to the opposite end of the railway's lifespan. Pier Head was understanably the busiest station on the Overhead as it provided connections with trams, buses and ferries. Between the staircases a notice reads 'Overhead Rly. To View Liners and Docks' but, prior to 1939, the latter part boasted 'Permits to View Liners Obtainable Here'. Round trip tickets were issued from 1926 and a special arrangement with the shipping companies allowed passengers to break journey and actually visit the ships at quayside. They were discontinued during the war and never reinstated, as wartime security in the docks was extended into peacetime. Austerity was still very much with us in 1956, an advertisement above the kiosk offering a stocking repair service!

1908 A fifty yard walk takes us to the foot of Water Street and we look back along that part of the thoroughfare known as George's Dock Gates. In the foreground, a policeman strides purposely towards Pier Head. He is sporting his summer issue straw helmet, commonly known as a 'donkey's breakfast'.

1910 The south end of Pier Head station, with a tempting display of fruit and confectionary available from the 'Cabin'.

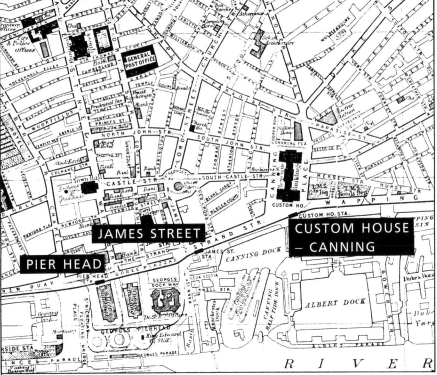

PIER HEAD

JAMES STREET

CUSTOM HOUSE
– CANNING

1948 An 0-4-0 saddle tank shunter rumbles cab first underneath Pier Head Station. Commonly called 'Pugs', these small engines were the mainstay of British Railways' labours along the waterfront for many years. Their short wheelbase made them ideal for the sharp curves of dockland lines.

1956 Pier Head ticket-collector, Mr Ryan. By now, the threatened closure of the railway is the only topic of conversation. Ticket stocks have been so run down that blanks with handwritten destinations have become a regular issue.

1930's Pier Head Station with a view to the north. The fully covered platforms denote an important station.

1956 Crossing to the 'up' platform, a 3-car set 19-16-7 arrives at the opposite platform with a service to Seaforth and Litherland.

1950 A street level view of the Overhead as a train leaves Pier Head.

1947 Looking back along the Goree warehouses from James Street. The warehouses were badly damaged during the war and were pulled down in the 1950's.

1930's Looking from Mann Island towards James Street offers a fine view of the fourth and final bow-string bridge on the system. Beyond the bridge are the offices of the White Star Line, with the Goree warehouses on the left. An advertising hoarding fixed to the Overhead structure offers: 'Easter and Whit Holidays Cruising – Atlantic Line "Doric" – From £5 White Star Line'.

1956 The small group of people descending from the 'up' platform indicate a train has just passed through to Dingle. A sign above their heads states 'Trains to Dingle and the South – Closed on Sundays'.

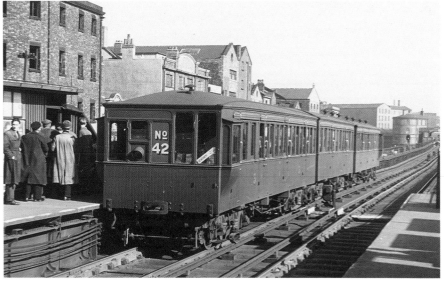

1950's Looking north from James Street. Passengers for Wirral could change here for the Mersey Railway station of the same name.

1950 Underway in a Southbound train of original stock. The next station, Canning, can be seen in the distance.

1950's Canning Station was originally named Custom House because of its proximity to the excise building. It was renamed in 1945 to end confusion amongst travellers after bomb damage, in 1940, forced Customs and Excise to relocate their offices. The remains of John Foster's magnificent building were finally pulled down in 1949.

1957 Canning's frontage viewed from Strand Street. The station was opposite Canning Place although the original quadrangle stood north of an imaginary line from Hanover Street to the docks, not south as does its present day namesake.

c.1908 Back on the 'up' platform and the view to the north shows the bustle of everyday city traffic.

1950's The next station is Wapping. The view from the rear coach shows the rebuilt shelters following wartime damage.

1956 A modernised unit brings us to the rebuilt Brunswick Dock Station.

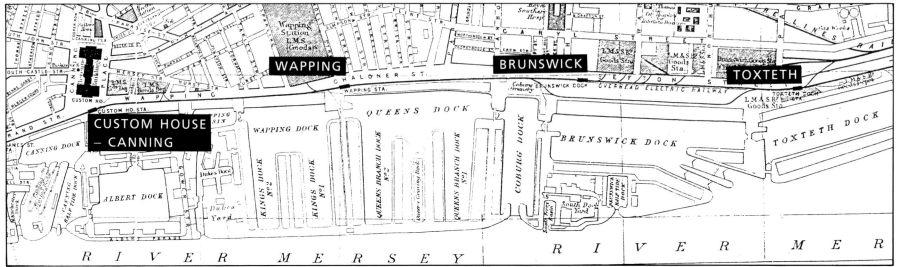

1931 A test opening of the Brunswick lift-bridge. Normally these operations were carried out after traffic had ceased for the day if abnormal loads required passage to or from the dock estate. Once the track fishplates had been disconnected, the bridge was raised by hydraulic rams housed in the supporting columns. There were three such structures on the Overhead, the other two being near Langton and Sandon Docks.

1930's Brunswick station prior to the actions of the Luftwaffe.

1930's Toxteth Station, with its similarity to Brunswick. The landward side is dominated by the Cheshire Lines Committee Railway's Brunswick goods station, its warehouse being visible in the background.

1956 Looking north from the platforms at Herculaneum (New) Station. The curved decking plates which precipitated the line's closure can be clearly seen together with occasional arched reinforcements.

1938 Taking the high ground at Grafton Street offers a view across the rails of the Cheshire Lines Committee. Below is the Brunswick engine shed, built in 1879. The depot reduced crowding at two smaller sheds nearby which serviced locomotives working to Brunswick Dock or Liverpool Central. LNER engines dominate the scene but LMS classes are also in evidence.

1950's Herculaneum from the junction of Grafton and Netherby Streets. The old station, a carriage shed since the Dingle extension, can be seen to good effect top left. The 200 foot lattice girder bridge which will plunge us underground on our final leg of the journey is visible on the right.

1930's Looking south to the Cheshire Lines and Overhead tunnels, which cross further inland. The latter's clearance above the former was only 33 inches and the treacherous sandstone rock necessitated delicate and costly engineering works during excavation.

1950's An unofficial walk along the structure from the 'new' station offers a closer inspection of the old terminus.

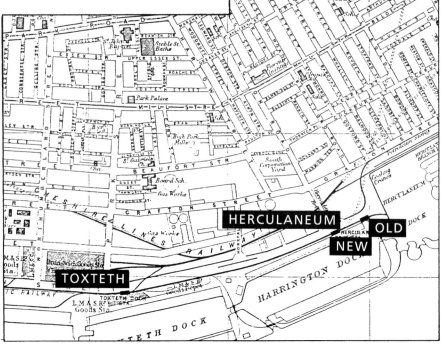

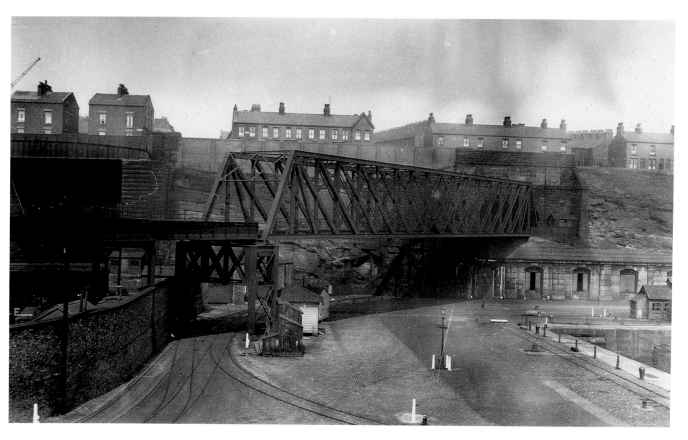

1938 An open window in the carriage shed frames the girder bridge at an angle rarely seen by members of the public.

1930's The last leg of the journey to Dingle. Rounding the curve, the lattice girder bridge looms high as the train heads for the darkness beyond.

1956 Once in the tunnel, there is little else to do but look around the dimly lit carriage, in this case, third class original stock.

1956 The more fortunate passenger would travel in a modernised third class compartment, with upholstered seating and electrically operated sliding doors.

1956 The hiss of air-brakes heralds our arrival at Dingle. The train enters the 'down' platform ready for the trip back to Seaforth in three minutes time.

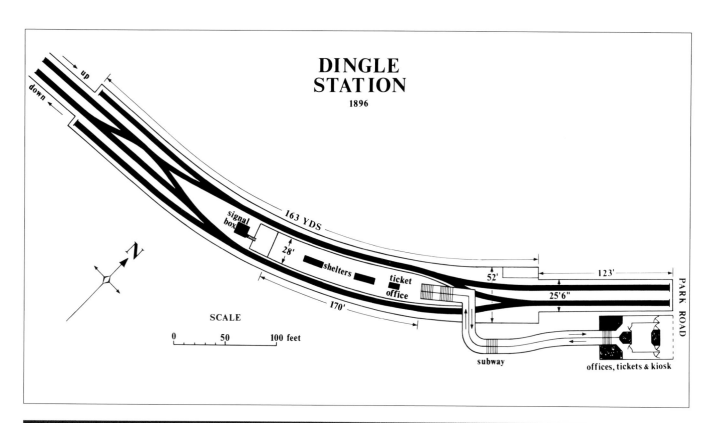

DINGLE STATION
1896

up

down

163 YDS

signal box

28'

shelters

ticket office

52'

123'

25'6"

170'

PARK ROAD

SCALE

0   50   100 feet

subway

offices, tickets & kiosk

N

1930's Dingle Station was the scene of the Overhead's worst disaster. In December, 1901, an electrical fire on board an incoming train got out of control and, fanned by the tunnel draught, quickly engulfed the terminus. Six people died and such was the devastation that Herculaneum deputised for more than a year afterwards.

1951 Dingle Station exit to Park Road and the end of a memorable journey.

AINTREE

Apart from the Grand National through traffic of LOR trains, Linacre Road and Ford stations saw regular week-day services between Aintree and Liverpool Exchange (via Marsh Lane and Strand Road) up to closure in 1951. The LYR Gladstone Dock station closed in 1924 after only 10 years service and Racecourse station was only used once a year hosting Grand National 'Specials' from all over the LYR network.

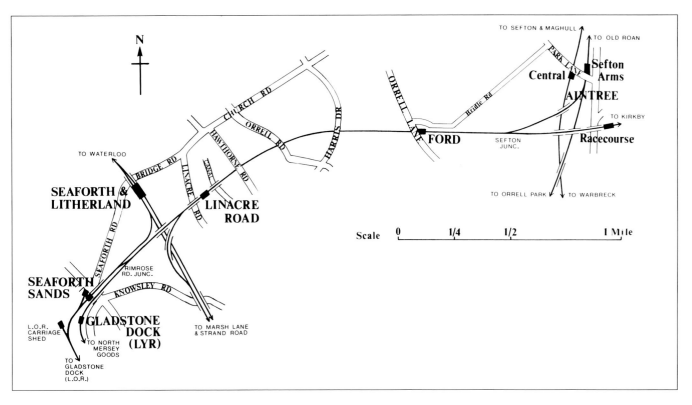

Crowds of racegoers from an Overhead train at Aintree in March, 1932.

Aintree Sefton Arms in the 1930's, with Overhead 3-car set 23-11-21 at platform 3. This and platform 4 (visible left) were only used for race meetings after regular services from the Southport line were curtailed in 1951.

Having disgorged its passengers for the 1956 Grand National, Overhead train 25-10-27 gets the 'all clear' from the guard to depart Aintree. Note the car numbers stencilled to the inside of the carriage door.

A view of BR and LOR trains approaching Aintree Sefton Arms, as seen from Park Lane bridge in 1956. The Overhead train (right) is dwarfed by the six coach service ex-Liverpool Exchange.

GRAND NATIONAL

SATURDAY, 24th, MARCH, 1956.

TRAVEL BY

OVERHEAD RAILWAY

WITHOUT CHANGING

DIRECT TO **AINTREE** RACECOURSE

		a.m.	a.m.	p.m.	p.m.	p.m.	p.m.	p.m.	p.m.	p.m.	p.m.
DINGLE	dep.	11 25	11 41	12 25	12 35	1 5	1 14	1 23	1 37	1 54	
JAMES STREET	"	11 35	11 50	12 35	12 45	1 15	1 24	1 33	1 47	2 4	
PIER HEAD	"	11 37	11 52	12 37	12 47	1 17	1 26	1 35	1 49	2 6	
SEAFORTH SANDS	"	11 53	12 8	12 53	1 3	1 33	1 42	1 53	2 8	2 23	
AINTREE (No. 1 Platform)	arr.	12 2	12 16	1 1	1 13	1 41	1 52	2 3	2 18	2 34	

		p.m.	p.m.	p.m.	p.m.	p.m.	p.m.	p.m.
AINTREE	dep.	3 50	4 7	4 24	4 42	4 51	5 1	5 31
SEAFORTH SANDS	"	4 4	4 19	4 34	4 51	5 4	5 12	5 41
PIER HEAD	"	4 18	4 33	4 48	5 5	5 18	5 26	5 55
JAMES STREET	"	4 19	4 34	4 49	5 6	5 19	5 27	5 56
DINGLE	arr.	4 28	4 43	4 58	5 15	5 28	5 36	6 5

DINGLE HERCULANEUM DK. TOXTETH DK. BRUNSWICK DK. WAPPING DK. CANNING DK. JAMES ST. PIER HEAD NELSON DK. CLARENCE DK. CANADA DK. HUSKISSON DK. ALEXANDRA DK. BROCKLEBANK DK. GLADSTONE DK. SEAFORTH L.M.R. for Southport SEAFORTH SANDS AINTREE L.M.R.

FARES from	Single	Return
DINGLE, HERCULANEUM, TOXTETH, BRUNSWICK, WAPPING and CANNING	1/-	2/-
JAMES STREET PIER HEAD CLARENCE, NELSON HUSKISSON CANADA, BROCKLEBANK, and ALEXANDRA	10D	1/8
GLADSTONE SEAFORTH SANDS	6D	1/-

The issuing of Through Tickets is subject to the conditions and regulations referred to in the Time Tables, Bills, and Notices of the respective Companies on whose Railways, Coaches or Steamboats they are available, and the holder, by accepting a Through Ticket agrees that the respective Companies are not to be liable for any loss or damage, injury, delay or detention caused or arising off their respective Railways Coaches or Steamboats. The Contract and liability of each Company are limited to its own Railway, Coaches or Steamboats.

Hargreaves Building, 5, Chapel Street, Liverpool, 3. March, 1956.

H. MAXWELL ROSTRON, General Manager & Engineer.

Save Time

Save Money

THE

OVERHEAD

IS STILL THE CHEAPEST TRANSPORT

TO THE CITY

Study these Fares

	THIRD CLASS	
DINGLE to PIER HEAD	4D SINGLE	7D RETURN

Season Tickets - Unlimited Journeys

	THIRD CLASS	
	WEEKLY	MONTHLY
DINGLE to PIER HEAD	4/9	18/-

First Class Extra - - - - Children Reduced Fares

FREQUENT & PUNCTUAL SERVICE

March, 1930, with an Overhead service ex-Aintree trundling past Ford Station en route to its own metals. This view from Orrell Lane shows the Aintree sorting sidings top right.

Rimrose Road Junction from the signal box in the 1930's sees an Overhead train crossing from LMS lines on its way back to Seaforth Sands. The route to Seaforth and Litherland is sloping away to the left.

A handbill advertising the company's last excursions to Aintree in 1956. It is curious that 'down' journey times between Seaforth Sands and Aintree varied from eight to ten minutes whilst equivalent returns took anything from nine to fourteen minutes.

THE LIVERPOOL OVERHEAD RAILWAY TRAMWAY

The Overhead operated an electric tramway which connected their terminus at Seaforth Sands with Crosby village, a distance of two and a half miles.

Services to 'Five Lamps' (Great Georges Road) began on June 9th, 1900 – extending to Crosby (Victoria Road) in October that year. The single track route followed Crosby Road South, Crosby Road North, Liverpool Road and Cooks Road. Initially, there were passing loops at fourteen points: Henley Street, Church Road, Lathom Avenue, Durham Road, Kinross Road, Great Georges Road, South Road, St Johns Road, Marldon Avenue, Myers Road West, Endbutt Lane, Coronation Road, Little Crosby Road and Victoria Road.

After 1906, rationalisation reduced the loops to nine; those at Henley Street, Myers Road West, Little Crosby Road and Victoria Road were removed and the loops at Kinross Road, Durham Road and Lathom Avenue were replaced by two new ones at Cambridge Road and Claremont Road.

The original rolling stock consisted of fourteen vehicles of three different types operating every six minutes during the day, except for Sunday mornings when twelve minute intervals were observed. The through journey lasted sixteen minutes with cars passing each other at Church Road, Cambridge Road, South Road, Marldon Avenue and Endbutt Lane. The other loops were only used when irregularities crept into the service.

By 1925, the condition of the trackwork was poor, resulting in noisy and uncomfortable journeys. The company's lease of the route was to terminate at the end of that year, having beeen refused an extension. A proposal to incorporate the service into Liverpool Corporation's fold failed and the last trams operated on December 31, 1925.

Motor buses of the Waterloo and Crosby Motor Services then plied the route until takeover by Ribble Motor Services in January, 1931.

The original 'Five Lamps' tram station (Great Georges Road) with northbound car 5 waiting in the passing loop.

Car 14 for Seaforth draws to a halt in the South Road loop, towards the end of the tramway's existence. The shelter on the left (which survives today on nearby allotments) displays Overhead services including a connection for 'Eastham Ferry and Gardens'.

Seaforth Sands station and tramshed from Arthur Street c.1910, with Overhead tram number 2.

A close-up of Seaforth tramshed in 1923 as viewed from the Caradoc public house (note MacLachlan's kiosk on the left and the National Telephone Company booths beyond).

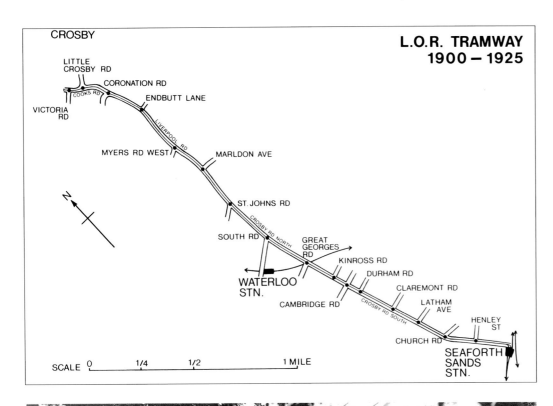

CROSBY

**L.O.R. TRAMWAY
1900 – 1925**

LITTLE
CROSBY RD

CORONATION RD

COOKS RD

ENDBUTT LANE

VICTORIA
RD

LIVERPOOL RD

MYERS RD WEST

MARLDON AVE

ST. JOHNS RD

CROSBY RD NORTH

SOUTH RD

GREAT
GEORGES
RD

KINROSS RD

DURHAM RD

WATERLOO
STN.

CAMBRIDGE RD

CROSBY RD SOUTH

CLAREMONT RD

LATHAM
AVE

HENLEY
ST

CHURCH RD

SEAFORTH
SANDS
STN.

SCALE 0   1/4   1/2   1 MILE

FRAM TERMINUS   GREAT CROSBY

Journey's end: Crosby terminus with car 4 receiving admiring glances from Mr Alcock's delivery boys. Victoria Road veers off to the left.

Above and opposite, a panoramic view of Seaforth Sands from the railway bridge in the late 1920's. The Waterloo and Crosby Motor Services buses which replaced the tram service mingle with single-decker coaches for Formby and Southport.

A joint LOR/WCMS handbill from 1926 giving details of through services.

THE LIVERPOOL OVERHEAD RAILWAY

AND

WATERLOO AND CROSBY MOTOR SERVICES, LTD.

CHEAP THROUGH RETURN TICKETS

ISSUED ALL DAY

	1st CLASS Return	3rd CLASS Return
Great Crosby to Pier Head, James St. or Custom House -	9 d.	7 d.
Waterloo to Pier Head, James St. or St John's Road Custom House -	8 d.	6 d.
By BUS and OVERHEAD RAILWAY Seaforth Sands to Pier Head or James St. -	6 d.	4 d.

On SATURDAYS (after 12 noon) SUNDAYS and BANK HOLIDAYS

Pier Head to Seaforth Sands -	6 d.	4 d.
Dingle, to or from Pier Head or James St. -	5 d.	3½ d.
Dingle, ,, ,, Seaforth Sands -	7½ d.	6 d.

WEEKDAYS (from 10 a.m.)

Dingle to James Street or Pier Head -	5 d.	3½ d.

These Tickets are not available at intermediate Stations. Return same day

SUNDAYS

AT SINGLE FARE FOR DOUBLE JOURNEY FROM ANY STATION

Children above 3 and under 12 years of age. Half Fare

FOR A GOOD VIEW OF DOCKS AND SHIPS

BOOK A CHEAP ROUND TRIP TICKET

From PIER HEAD or JAMES STREET to DINGLE or SEAFORTH SANDS and BACK AGAIN

Week Days - - - -	1/-	9 d.
Saturday Afternoon and Sunday -	7½ d.	6 d.

Apply 31, James Street, Liverpool
May, 1926   E. J. NEACHELL

PLEASE RETAIN THIS BILL FOR REFERENCE   [P.T.O.

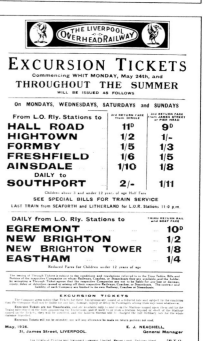

THE LIVERPOOL OVERHEAD RAILWAY

EXCURSION TICKETS

Commencing WHIT MONDAY, May 24th, and

THROUGHOUT THE SUMMER

WILL BE ISSUED AS FOLLOWS

On MONDAYS, WEDNESDAYS, SATURDAYS and SUNDAYS

From L.O. Rly. Stations to	3rd RETURN FARE from DINGLE	3rd RETURN FARE from JAMES STREET or PIER HEAD
HALL ROAD	11ᴰ	9ᴰ
HIGHTOWN	1/2	1/-
FORMBY	1/5	1/3
FRESHFIELD	1/6	1/5
AINSDALE	1/10	1/8
DAILY to SOUTHPORT	2/-	1/11

Children above 3 and under 12 years of age Half Fare

SEE SPECIAL BILLS FOR TRAIN SERVICE

LAST TRAIN from SEAFORTH and LITHERLAND for L.O.R. Stations 11·0 p.m.

DAILY from L.O. Rly. Stations to	THIRD RETURN RAIL and BOAT FARE
EGREMONT	10ᴰ
NEW BRIGHTON	1/2
NEW BRIGHTON TOWER	1/8
EASTHAM	1/4

Reduced Fares for Children under 12 years of age

The issuing of Through Tickets is subject to the conditions and regulations referred to in the Time Tables, Bills and Notices of the respective Companies on whose Railways, Coaches, or Steamboats they are available, and the holder, by accepting a Through Ticket agrees that the respective Companies are not to be liable for any loss or damage, injury, delay or detention caused or arising off their respective Railways, Coaches, or Steamboats. The contract and liability of each Company are limited to its own Railway, Coaches or Steamboats.

EXCURSION TICKETS

The Company gives notice that Tickets for these Excursions are issued at a reduced rate and subject to the conditions that the Company shall not be liable for any loss, damage, injury of delay to Passengers arising from any cause whatever.

Excursion Tickets are not Transferable, and are available only to and along the Stations named upon them and by the Trains advertised with the Bills concerning the Excursions, and if used to or from a station beyond or short of the Stations named on the Tickets, they will be forfeited, and the holders thereof will be charged the full ordinary fare for the whole distance travelled.

Excursion Tickets will not be extended, nor will any allowance be made on return portions not used.

May, 1926.   E. J. NEACHELL,
31, James Street, LIVERPOOL.   General Manager

The Liverpool Printing and Stationery Company Limited Manchester Buildings Street   [P.T.O.

BUILDING and DEMOLITION

Reproduced from 'Engineering' (December, 1891), this view shows the ingenious method employed erecting spans on the Overhead. Rails at three levels contributed to the assembly of each new deck; the front forks of the contraption were guided by ground level track while the rear bow-legs were supported by rail laid on the previous section. Next, travelling cranes above manoeuvred the decks into position. Once rails had been fitted to the latest span, the whole apparatus moved forward ready for the next decking to be rolled into place and eased through the bow-legs by the cranes. The spans travelled on the Overhead by special trolley from their assembly point near Seaforth. Progress was approximately two sections a day, the average span being fifty feet in length.

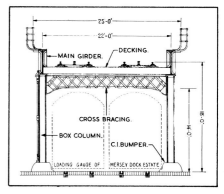

A cross section of the elevated structure showing dimensions.

Work proceeding south towards Alexandra, in 1891, with proud Ives and Barker employees grouping for the photograph.

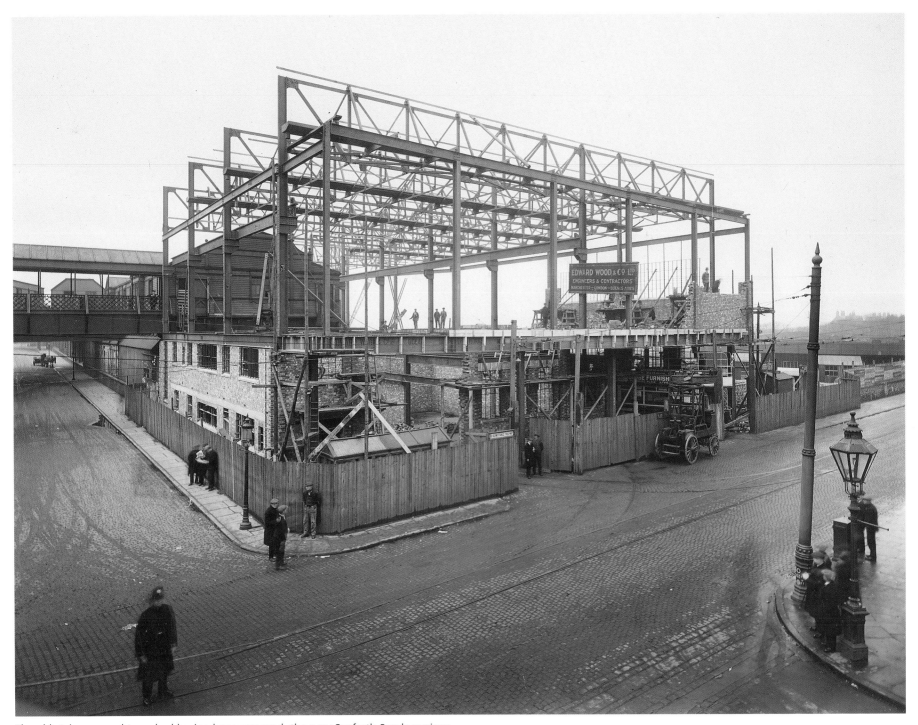

The old staircases and tramshed having been removed, the new Seaforth Sands carriage
shed takes shape, as seen from the Seaforth Road embankment in April, 1925.

By August, 1925, only the skeleton of Seaforth Sands terminus remained, as work on the new building progressed to track level.

The first sections of the Overhead to be dismembered were just north of Herculaneum. This September, 1957, photograph testifies to the modus operandi, which was to use cutters aided by mobile crane, effective but crude compared with the elegant method of construction described earlier. Note the floating crane 'Samson' in Harrrington Dock to the left.

A contractor's train heading south in October, 1957, to collect more rails for scrap.

In a scene reminiscent of the Blitz, the fine canopies at Pier Head Station succumb to a demolition team in November, 1957.

The carcass of Canning Station immediately prior to felling in April, 1958.

Piece by piece, an institution disappears. Columns resembling trees stand guard in Wapping while a precariously stacked pile of decking plates await removal by road in April, 1958.

A last look at the remains of Pier Head Station and its bow-string bridges (April, 1958). The 'Cabin' kiosk is shuttered up and even the corporation tramlines in front are redundant. By July, only a few columns were left.

After closure, rolling stock was stored between Seaforth Sands and Gladstone stations prior to scrapping. The photograph shows three rakes of modernised cars awaiting their fate.

MISCELLANY

The last Overhead Railway vehicle to see service, an Austin lorry GKD 148 seen here at Wapping with driver G McMahon (April, 1958).

In 1917, certain automatic 'home' signals were linked to electrically operated train-stops placed just ahead of the relevant signals. If a train went through a 'red' light, a contact brush on the vehicle was tripped by the cocked bar at the side of the inner rail (shown left). Contact automatically shut off current to the train and applied the air-brakes, bringing it safely to a halt. The right hand illustration shows the device in the uncocked position.

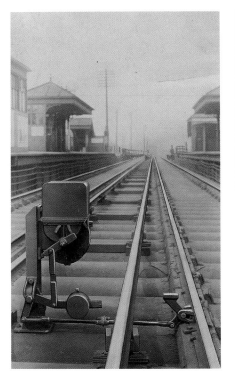

From the outset, the Overhead had a tiny Kitson engine for departmental purposes. It was used for hauling men and materials as well as clearing ice from the rails (note the cutters ahead of the leading wheels). Nicknamed 'Lively Polly' by the staff, it was sold in 1948, having been replaced by a Rushton diesel the previous year.

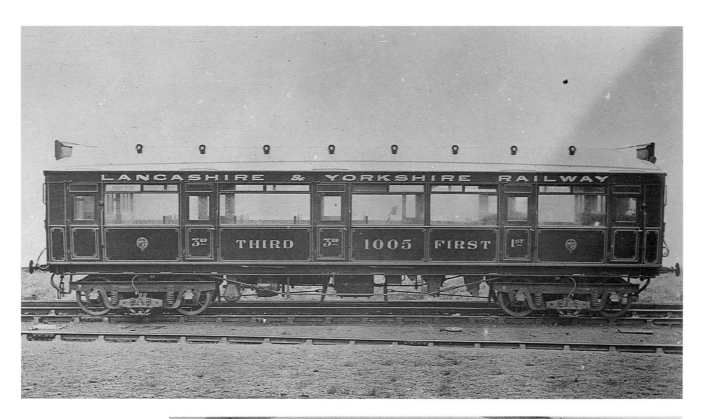

Exterior and interior views of one of the twelve Lancashire and Yorkshire Railway lightweight cars built for the through Southport to Dingle service introduced in 1906. The service was withdrawn in August, 1914, receipts not having lived up to the company's expectations. The vehicles then went to operate the Southport/Crossens service but returned each year until the outbreak of World War Two for Dingle/Aintree race traffic.

The single platformed LYR Gladstone Dock Station was opened in September, 1914, as a satellite branch from the company's Aintree – Marsh lane – Liverpool Exchange service. Constructed entirely of wood and clinging to a curved viaduct, its entrance was in Shore Road. The station was closed by LMS in July, 1924, having being found an unremunerative extravagence. Note the proximity of Seaforth Sands in the background.

The Overhead's enquiry bureau during centenary celebrations of the Liverpol and Manchester Railway opening. Staged in Wavertree Playground, in 1930, visitors were invited to 'book a round trip and ask for a liner permit'. An employee, clearly cut out for the job, points to vessels 'Scythia', 'Adriatic' and 'Doric' being on view that day. The raised blackboard details the opportunities in the coming week, with columns dedicated to Cunard, White Star and Canadian Pacific ships.

A joint LOR/LMS handbill advertising day and half-day excursions to Southport for the 1925 season.

LIVERPOOL OVERHEAD
AND
LONDON, MIDLAND & SCOTTISH RAILWAYS

EXCURSIONS, DAY & HALF-DAY
ISSUED DAILY
May 2nd, until further notice

TO
SOUTHPORT
(CHAPEL STREET)

From	MONDAYS, TUESDAYS, THURSDAYS AND FRIDAYS											
	am	am	pm	pm	pm	pm	pm	pm	pm	pm	pm	p.m.
DINGLE	9 45	10 35	12 45	1 5	1 25	1 45	2 5	5 45	5 55	6 5	6 25	6 50
JAMES STREET	9 56	10 46	12 56	1 16	1 36	1 56	2 16	5 56	6 6	6 16	6 36	6 59
PIER HEAD	9 57	10 47	12 57	1 17	1 37	1 57	2 17	5 57	6 7	6 17	6 37	7 0

From	WEDNESDAYS AND SATURDAYS			SUNDAYS						
	am	am		pm	pm	pm	pm	pm	pm	pm
DINGLE	9 45	10 35	And Trains leaving Dingle	2 15	2 55	4 55	5 35	6 5	6 15	6 35
JAMES STREET	9 56	10 46	between 11 35 am and	—	—	—	—	—	—	—
PIER HEAD	9 57	10 47	6 35 pm (inclusive)	2 23	3 3	5 3	5 43	6 13	6 23	6 43

Returning from SOUTHPORT (Chapel Street) same day after 3-0 pm.

From James St. & Pier Head

RETURN FARE (THIRD CLASS) 1/11
Children above 3 and under 12 years of age HALF-FARE.

To HALL ROAD, HIGHTOWN, FORMBY, FRESHFIELD & AINSDALE
On MONDAYS, WEDNESDAYS, SATURDAYS and SUNDAYS

From	MONDAYS and WEDNESDAYS				SATURDAYS				SUNDAYS			RETURN FARES (3rd Class) to :—				
												HALL ROAD	HIGH-TOWN	FORMBY	FRESH-FIELD	AINS-DALE
	pm	pm	pm	pm	pm	pm	pm	pm	pm	pm	pm					
DINGLE	1 25	2 5	2 25	2 45	2 5	2 25	2 45	3 5	1 55	2 15	2 35	11d.	1/2	1/5	1/6	1/10
JAMES STREET	1 36	2 16	2 36	2 56	2 16	2 36	2 56	3 16	—	—	—	9d.	1/-	1/3	1/5	1/8
PIER HEAD	1 37	2 17	2 37	2 57	2 17	2 37	2 57	3 17	2 3	2 23	2 43					

Returning same day by any Ordinary Train after 3-0 pm.   Children above 3 and under 12 years of age HALF-FARE

The issuing of Through Tickets is subject to the conditions and regulations referred to in the Time Tables, Bills, and Notices of the respective Companies on whose Railways, Coaches, or Steamboats they are available, and the holder, by accepting a Through Ticket agrees that the respective Companies are not to be liable for any loss or damage, injury, delay, or detention caused or arising off their respective Railways, Coaches, or Steamboats. The contract and liability of each Company are limited to its own Railway, Coaches, or Steamboats.

31, JAMES STREET
LIVERPOOL, April 1925.

E. J. NEACHELL, General Manager, Overhead Railway.
H. G. BURGESS, General Manager, L. M. & S. Railway.

The Liverpool Printing and Stationery Company Limited, Mercer Court, Redcross Street